WHS

national TESTS
practice papers

FOR THE YEAR 2002

Year 4 Optional Tests

Maths

practice Papers

AGE

8-9

Year 4

First published 2001
exclusively for WHSmith by

Hodder & Stoughton Educational,
a division of Hodder Headline Ltd
338 Euston Road
London NW1 3BH

A CIP record for this book is available from the British Library.

Authors: Steve Mills and Hilary Koll

ISBN 0340 84595 3

Printed and bound by Graphycems, Spain

NOTE: The tests, questions and advice in this book are not reproductions of the official test materials sent to schools. The official testing process is supported by guidance and training for teachers in setting and marking tests and interpreting the results. The results achieved in the tests in this book may not be the same as are achieved in the official tests.

Contents

Introduction

The National Tests: A Summary

What are the National Tests?

Children who attend state schools in England and Wales sit National Tests (also known as SATs) at the ages of 7, 11 and 14, usually at the beginning of May. They may also sit optional tests in the intervening years – many schools have chosen to adopt these tests. The test results are accompanied by an assessment by the child's teacher (at Key Stage 3 this also covers non-tested subjects such as History or Geography).

The results are used by the school to assess each child's level of knowledge and progress in English and Maths at Key Stage 1 and English, Maths and Science at Key Stages 2 and 3. They also provide useful guidance for the child's next teacher when he or she is planning the year's work.

The educational calendar for children aged 5-14 is structured as follows:

Key Stage	Year	Age by end of year	National Test
1 (KS1)	1	6	
	2	7	KEY STAGE 1
2 (KS2)	3	8	Optional Year 3
	4	9	Optional Year 4
	5	10	Optional Year 5
	6	11	KEY STAGE 2
3 (KS3)	7	12	
	8	13	
	9	14	KEY STAGE 3

Test Timetable

The Key Stage 1 National Tests are carried out in **May**. They often form part of children's normal school day, as they are generally practical and teacher-assessed. Many children at Key Stage 1 do not even realise they are taking a test.

Key Stage 2 tests take place in one week in May. All children sit the same test at the same time. In 2002, the tests will take place in the week of **13–17 May**. Your child's school will be able to provide you with a detailed timetable.

Key Stage 3 students will sit their tests on **7–13 May.**

Levels

National average levels have been set for children's results in the National Tests. The levels are as follows:

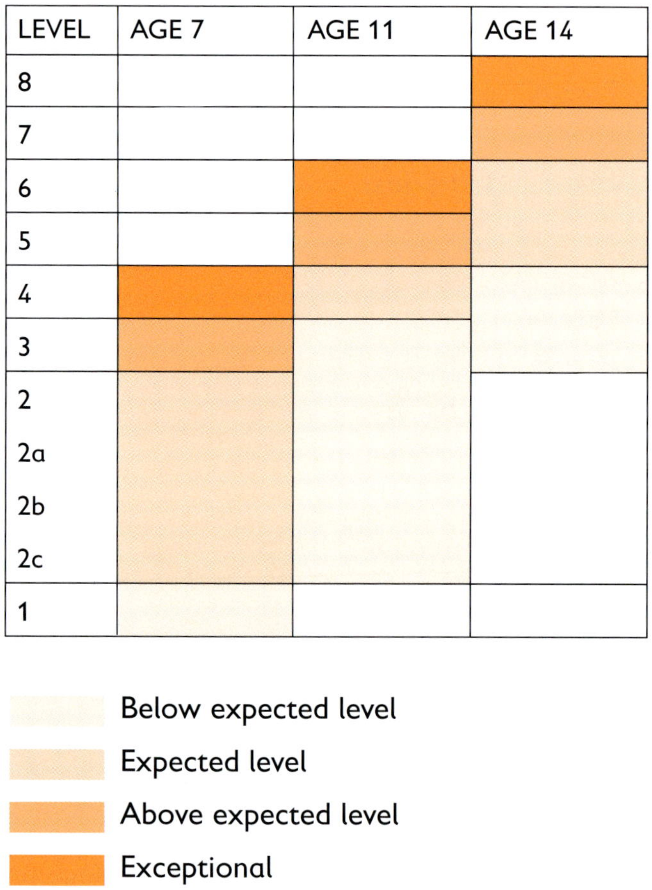

Results

Your child's school will send you a report indicating his or her levels in the tests and the teacher assessment.

The school's overall test results will be included in local and national league tables, which are published in most newspapers.

What can parents do to help?

While it is never a good idea to encourage cramming, you can help your child to succeed by:

- Making sure he or she has enough food, sleep and leisure time during the test period.
- Practising important skills such as writing and reading stories, spelling and mental arithmetic.
- Telling him or her what to expect in the test, such as important symbols and key words.
- Helping him or her to be comfortable in test conditions including working within a time limit, reading questions carefully and understanding different ways of answering.

Maths at Year 4

Typical 7 year-olds attain Level 2 in Maths at the end of Year 2. By the end of Year 4, most children will be working towards Level 3. Some might be attaining a Level 3 and some very able children might attain Level 4.

Setting the test

The written test

Allow between 45 minutes and one hour to complete the written test. If your child attempts Part B, allow longer.

Your child will need a ruler, pencil, rubber and, if possible, a small mirror or piece of tracing paper. No extra writing paper is needed. Calculators must not be used.

The written test is split into two parts, A and B. If your child scores highly in Part A, he or she can go on to try the harder questions in Part B. There is not a strict time limit on this test, but do not force your child to continue if he or she can no longer answer any questions.

If your child has difficulty in reading the questions, these can be read aloud, provided the mathematical words are not altered or explained. Where necessary, children can dictate their answers for you to write them down. For large numbers, however, a child should be clear which digits are intended to be written, e.g. for a number such as three thousand and six the child must indicate that this should be written three, zero, zero, six.

The mental test

The marks scored in the national mental mathematics test are not included when levelling at Year 4. However, in the Year 6 National Tests your child's mental scores will form part of the overall mark used for levelling.

The mental test should take approximately 10–15 minutes to give, and it is necessary for you to read aloud the questions on pages 25 and 26. Cut these pages out for this purpose. Your child will only need a pencil and rubber for the mental test.

The mental test contains a series of questions for you to read to your child and answer sheets for him or her to write answers on. Allow only the time suggested for each question and read each question twice.

Marking the tests

Next to each question is a number indicating how many marks the question or part of the question is worth. Enter your child's mark into the circle, using the answer pages to help you decide how many points to award.

Find your child's total score from the written test and refer to page 34 for information about the level your child might be working at.

Practice pages

At the end of the book are some practice pages to boost your children's skills even further.

Maths Test
Part A

1 Look at these cards.

+	−	÷	=

Use these cards to make correct number sentences.

You can use a card more than once.

26 ☐ 9 ☐ 17 1

35 ☐ 5 ☐ 7 1

2 Leanne is planting **31** flowers in her garden.

After planting the **eleventh** flower, how many more has she left to plant? ☐ 1

TOTAL

3

Part A

3 How many

are worth the same as

?

1

4 Here are some birds on a branch.

A few minutes ago there were **twice** as many birds on this branch. How many birds were on the branch?

1

5 Fill in the missing numbers.

$76 + \bigcirc = 103$

$92 - \diamond = 38$

1

1

TOTAL

4

6 Write the number that is half way between these two numbers.

11	16	21

1

7 Count back in ones from 1005.

1005, 1004, 1003, ___, ___, ___, ___, ___, ___, ___, ___, ___, ___

1

TOTAL

2

Part A

8 This table shows the number of letters Mrs Jones received each day.

Day	Number of letters
Monday	2
Tuesday	4
Wednesday	6
Thursday	9
Friday	2
Saturday	7

On which two days did Mrs Jones get the **least** number of letters?

1

How many more letters did she get on Wednesday than on Friday?

1

What was the total number of letters Mrs Jones received during this week?

1

TOTAL

3

9 Round these numbers to the nearest ten by drawing a line to the correct circle.

73 67 84 62 75

60 70 80

1

10 Which of the shapes below is a reflection of the shaded shape? Tick your answer.

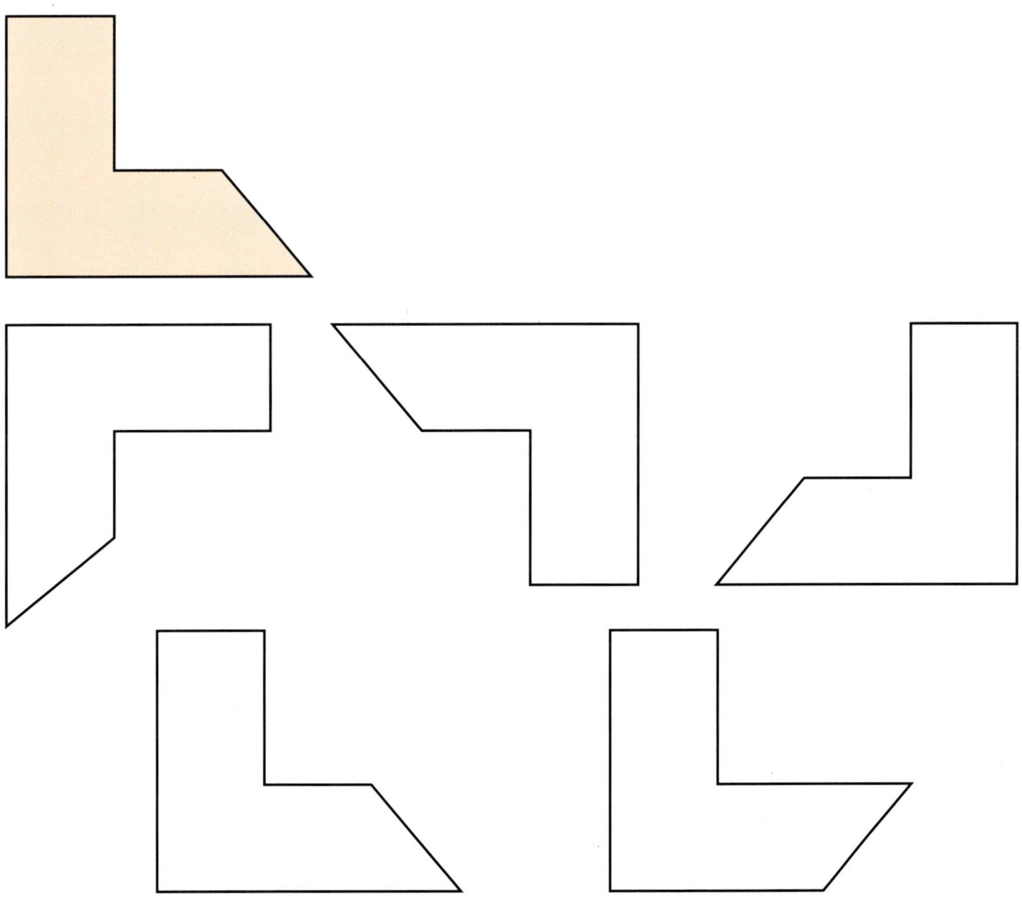

1

TOTAL

2

Part A

11 Fill in the missing spaces on this **tally chart**.

Number of shells some children collected from the beach

name	tally	number of shells
Jamilla	𝍸 |	6
Rumi	𝍸 𝍸 ||||	14
Dean	𝍸 𝍸 𝍸	15
Jasper	𝍸 ||	7
Sarah	𝍸 𝍸	10

1

How many shells were collected in total?

52

1

Part of this information has been drawn onto a graph. Finish the graph using the tally chart above.

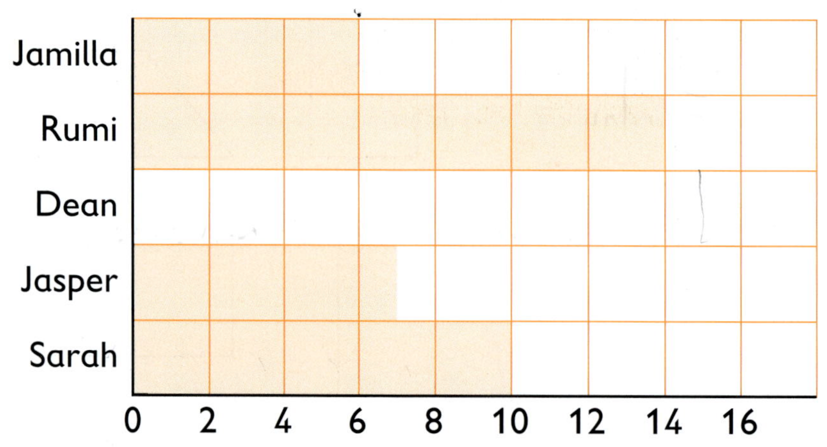

1

TOTAL

3

12 Shade **four** more squares to make this pattern symmetrical. You can use a mirror.

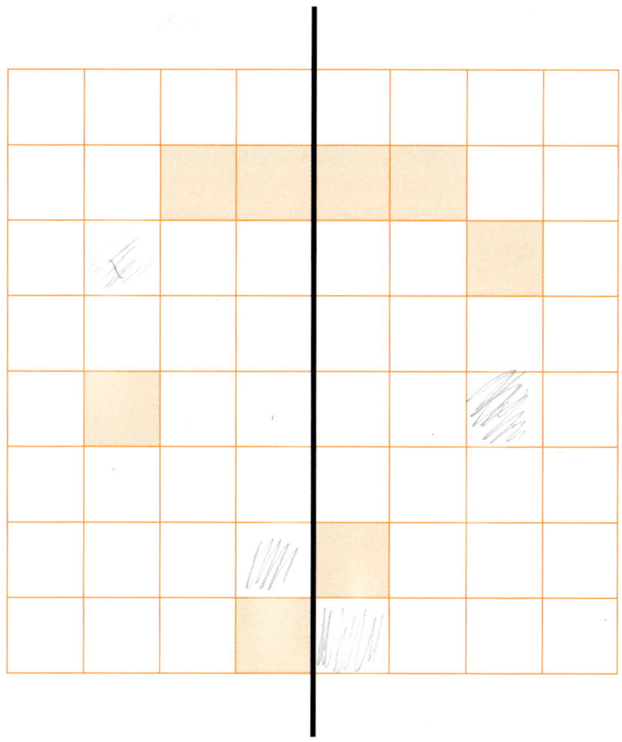

Mirror line

1

13

There are **136 adults** and **268 children** at the cinema. What is the total number of people?

1

TOTAL

2

Part A

14 Paul collects 38 acorns. He puts 13 in a jar and the rest onto a tray. How many acorns are on the tray?

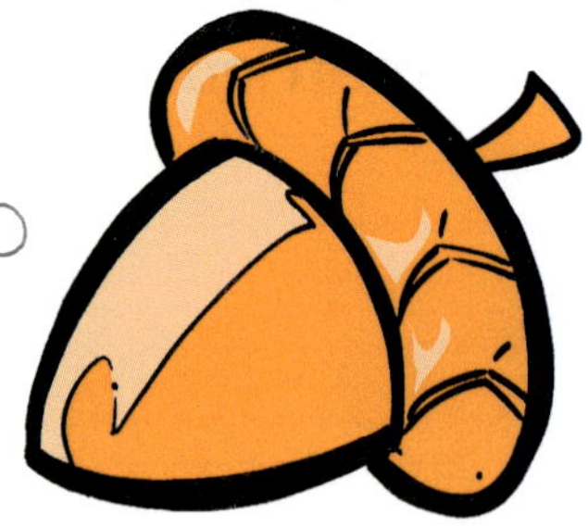

1

15 What is the mass of the potatoes?

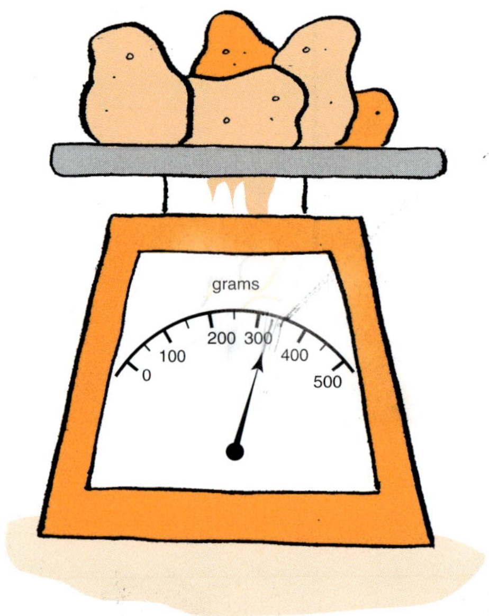

g

1

16 Write the answer.

$36 \div 4 =$

1

TOTAL

3

17 With a ruler, draw a line that is **half as long** as this line. 1

18 Draw a ring around **one fifth** of these drawing pins.

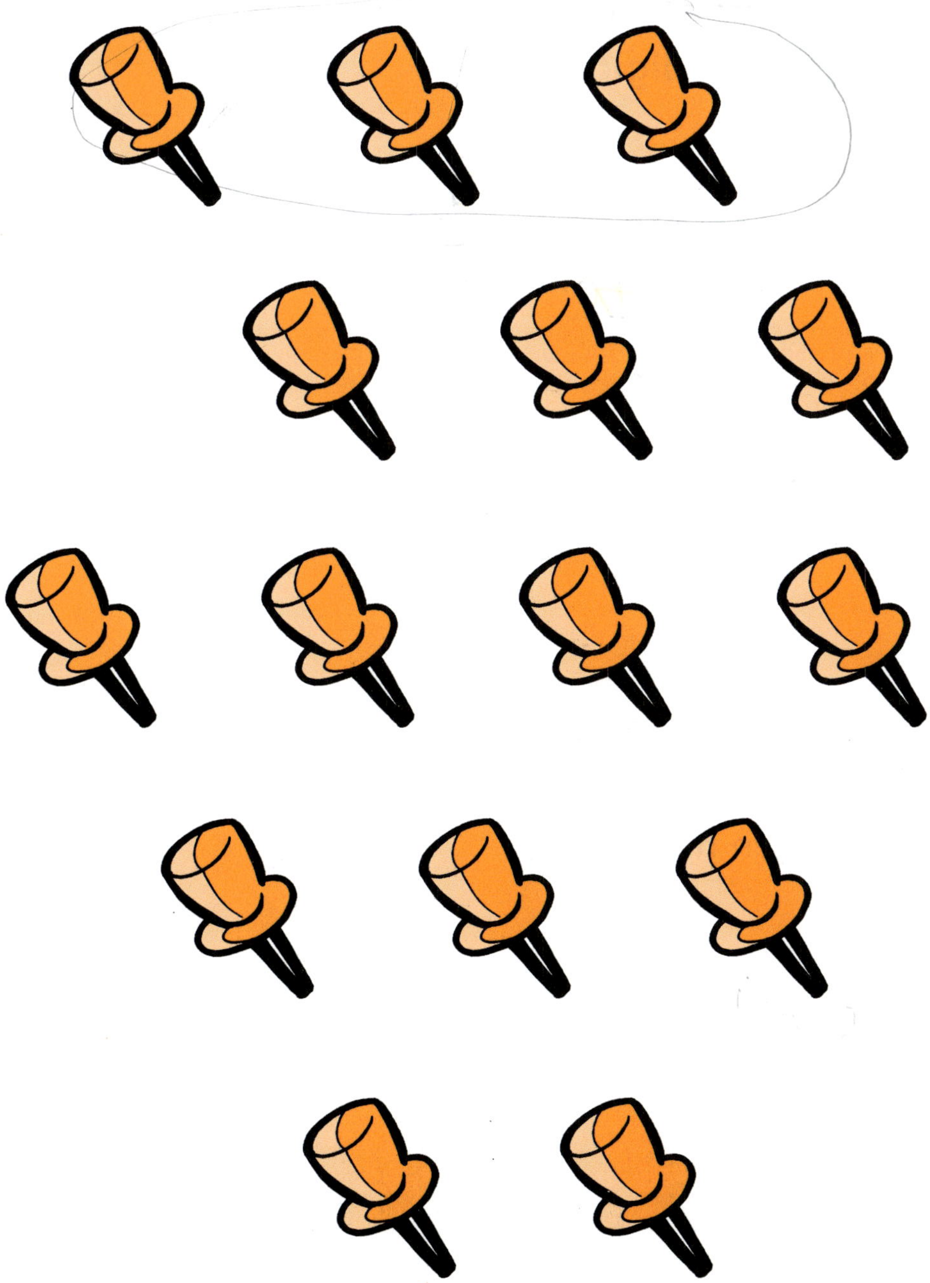

1

TOTAL

2

Part A

19 Use these digits to make some **four-digit** numbers.

6	9	5	7

Write the largest **four-digit** number. 9765

1

Write the smallest **four-digit** number. 5679

1

Write a number **exactly divisible by 5**. 6975

1

Write a number between 5000 and 7000. 6000

1

20 Add **435** to **369**.

Show your working in this box.

$$\begin{array}{r} 435 \\ +369 \\ \hline 804 \end{array}$$

1

TOTAL

5

21 Join each of these numbers to the nearest hundred.

	300
483	
	400
648	
	500
591	
	600
353	
	700

1

22 Camera films cost £5.09 for a pack of two.
How much would it cost to buy 6 films?

£

1

TOTAL

2

Part A

23 Continue this halving sequence.

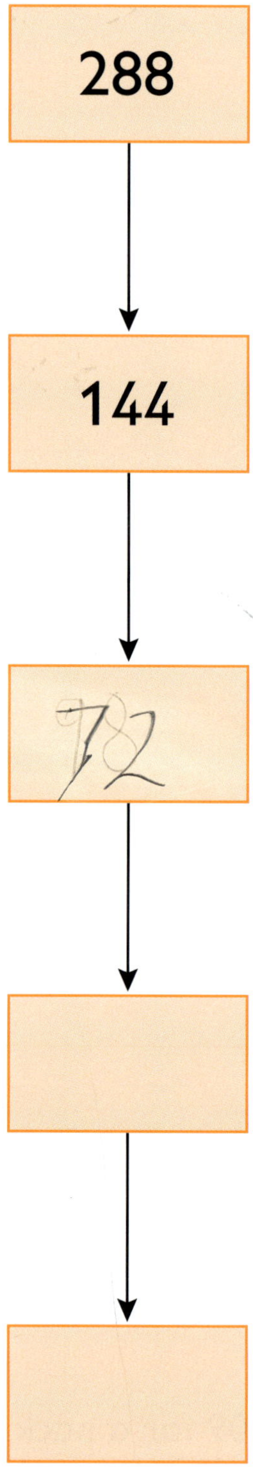

1

TOTAL

1

24 **5** pieces of wood, each **32 cm** long, are cut from a **2 m** wooden plank.

Which of these would you use to find how much wood is left over?

Tick your answer.

$5 + 32 + 2$	$5 \times 32 + 40$
$5 \times 32 - 2$ ✓	$200 - (5 \times 32)$ ✓
$5 \times 32 + 2$	$200 - (5 + 32)$

1

25 Answer this question.

$37 \times 100 =$ 3700

1

TOTAL

2

Part A

26 James has exactly **£7.60** in his money box.

He only collects **50p** and **20p** coins.

How many of each coin do you think he has?

[14] 50p coins and [36] 20p coins

1

27 Use a ruler to join dots to draw an **octagon** that has **at least one right angle.**

1

TOTAL

2

28 Match the time on Big Ben to one of the digital clocks with a line.

3:05

5:23

2:55

5:20

3:55

1

TOTAL

1

Part A

29 Join each answer to its matching question.

17	$19 + 9$
24	$34 - 17$
28	$37 + 9$
38	$40 - 16$
46	$28 + 15$
43	$52 - 14$

2

30 Shade one tenth of this grid.

1

31 How many full $\frac{1}{2}$ **litre** cups of water will it take to fill this jug?

1

TOTAL

4

32 One of these descriptions of this shape is correct.

Tick the correct description.

1

It is a pentagon with three right angles.

It is a symmetrical hexagon.

It is a hexagon with one right angle.

This shape does not have any right angles.

This shape is a hexagon with no right angles.

STOP HERE AND MARK PART A

TOTAL

1

Maths Test

Part B

33 Emma scored **141** with 3 darts.

Her first dart scored **57**.

Her second dart scored **48**.

How many did she score with her third dart?

Show your working in this box.

57 + 48 = 105

105 + 36 = 141

answer: 36

Well done

1

34 Complete this two-digit number to make a **multiple of 7**.

5	6

1

35 Write the number that is exactly **half way** between

2.6 and 3.2

2.9

1

TOTAL

3

36 One side of a square has been drawn on the grid.

Draw the other sides to finish the square.

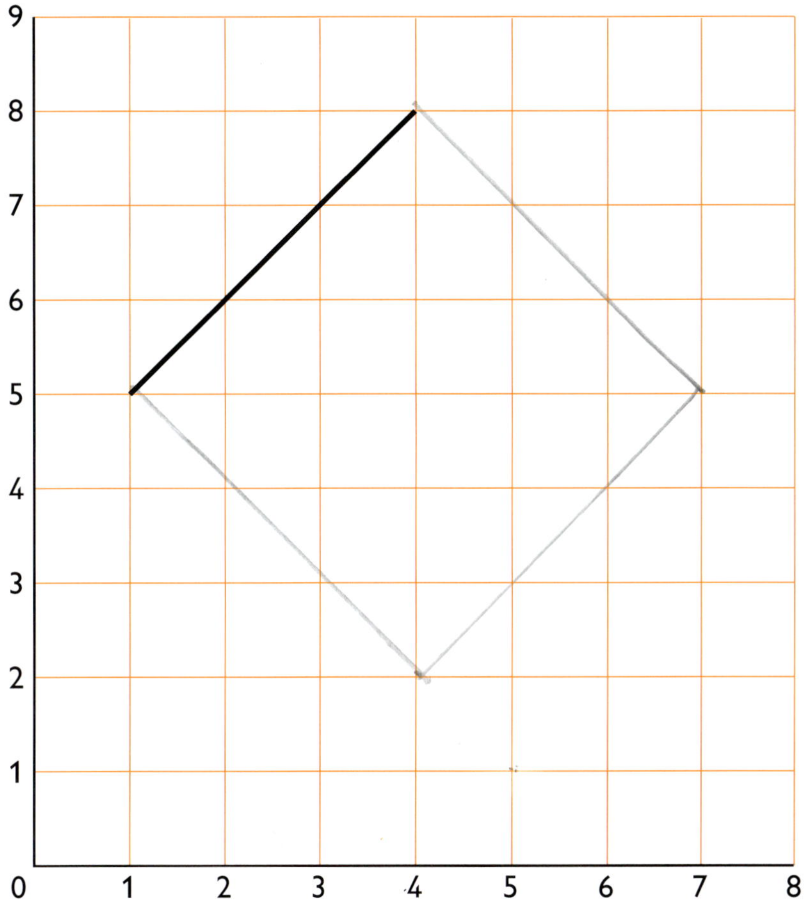

1

Write the co-ordinates of the corners of the square.

(4 , 2)	(7 , 5)	(4 , 8)	(1 , 5)

2

TOTAL

3

Part B

37 **4.7** is marked on this number line.

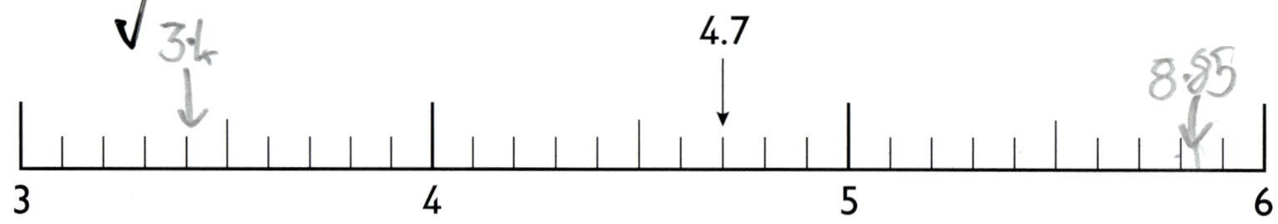

Mark **3.4** on the line. 1

Mark **5.85** on the line. 1

38 Write the missing numbers in the boxes.

Factors of 18 = | 1 | 2 | | | | | 1

TOTAL 3

39 Draw a ring around the amount this apple is most likely to weigh.

150 kg

10 kg

10 g

150 g

1500 g

150 kg

1

TOTAL

1

Part B

40 The street lights were lit on Wednesday at 21:36.

They went off on Thursday at 08:15.

How long were the lights on for?

hours	minutes

1

41 Write the correct number in the box.

37 − 29 = 24 ÷ 3

1

TOTAL

2

42 Write each of these letters in the correct region of this diagram.

X S M E

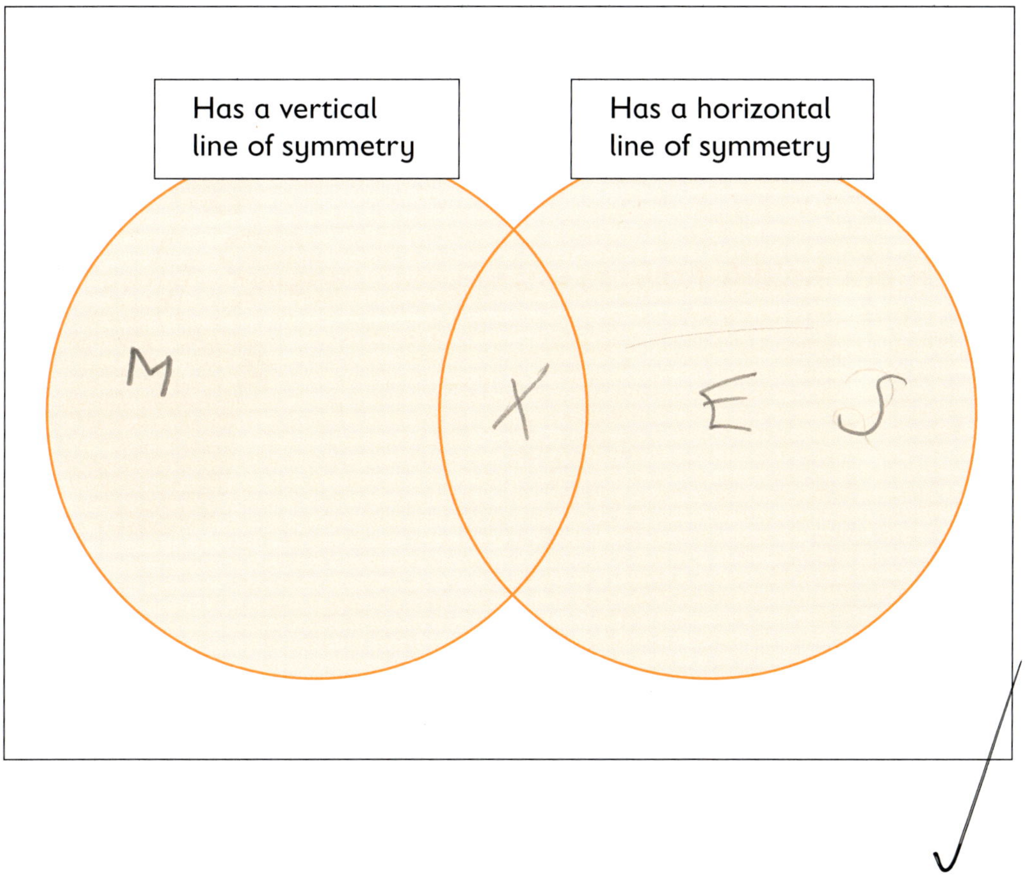

2

TOTAL

2

Part B

43 The **perimeter** of a rectangle is **26 cm.**

The **length** of one side is **6 cm**.

What is the **area** of the rectangle?

42cm²

1

44 Sanjay planted **62** flowers into pots.

Each pot held **4** flowers.

How many pots did he need?

1

How many pots were full?

1

TOTAL

3

"For this first set of questions you have five seconds to work out each answer and write it down."

1 What is double nine?

2 Three, six, nine... What comes next?

3 How many eight pence chews can you buy with twenty four pence?

4 Subtract eleven from thirty three.

5 Write an odd number between forty two and fifty.

6 Add one to nine hundred and ninety nine.

7 Sixty children get into teams of five. How many teams are there?

8 Multiply three by nine.

9 Write the number seven hundred and twelve in figures.

10 What is nought point six plus nought point five?

11 What is ten more than ninety six?

12 Pete had a five pound note. He spent three pounds and eighty pence. How much has he now?

Mental Maths Test

"For the next set of questions you have ten seconds to work out each answer and write it down."

13 Write two numbers that have a difference of sixteen.

14 Look at the answer sheet. How many small cubes have been joined to make this cuboid?

15 Look at the answer sheet. What is the perimeter of this pentagon?

16 What number is one quarter of forty eight?

17 How many centimetres are there in two and a half metres?

18 If two hundred sweets are shared equally between four people, how many sweets does each person get?

19 Circle the decimal that is equivalent to nine tenths.

20 I'm thinking of a number. I divide it by three. My answer is twenty. What is my number?

5-second questions

1		1
2		1
3		1
4		1
5		1
6		1
7		1
8		1
9		1
10	0.6 0.5	1
11		1
12		1

TOTAL

12

10-second questions

1	**13**	
1	**14**	
1	**15**	
1	**16**	
1	**17**	
1	**18**	
1	**19**	9.0 0.9 9.10 0.910 10.9
1	**20**	

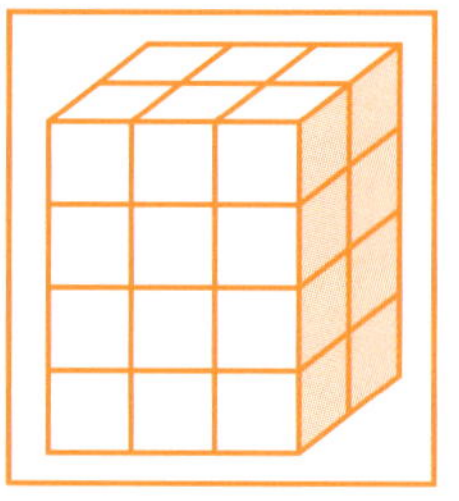

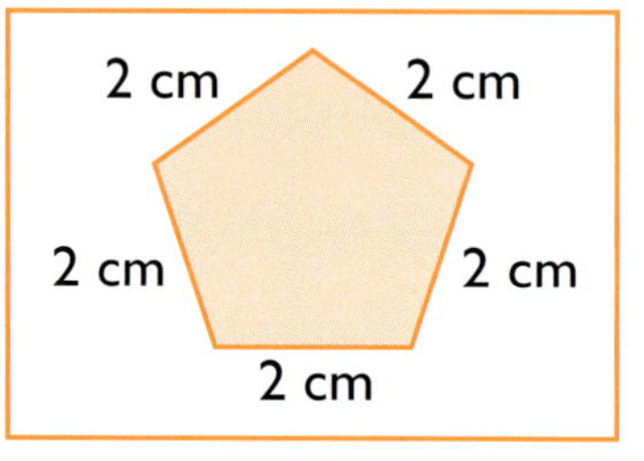

TOTAL

8

Answers

Part A

Question number	Answer	Mark	Parent's notes and additional comments
1a	26 − 9 = 17 *or* 26 = 9 + 17	1	
1b	35 ÷ 5 = 7	1	
2	20	1	
3	10	1	
4	18	1	
5a	76 + **27** = 103	1	Some children may make the mistake of adding 76 and 103. Children need to realise that despite having an addition sign, this question can be answered by subtracting 76 from 103.
5b	92 − **54** = 38	1	
6	16	1	A useful way of finding the number half way between two others is to add the two numbers, e.g. 11 and 21, and then halve the answer, e.g. 32 ÷ 2 = 16.
7	1005, 1004, 1003, **1002, 1001, 1000, 999, 998, 997, 996, 995, 994**	1	Some children find continuing the numbers either side of a multiple of 1000, e.g. 2000, 6000, 8000, quite difficult.
8a	Monday, Friday	1	Ask your child to read each number aloud to ensure he or she can read the numerals correctly.
8b	4	1	
8c	30	1	
9	73 → 70 67 → 70 84 → 80 62 → 60 75 → 80	1	Remind your child that numbers ending in 5 are rounded up.
10	The third shape: 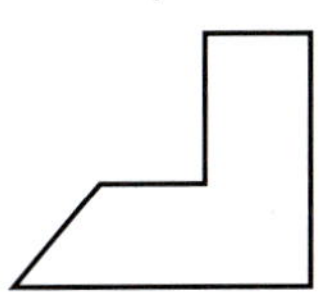	1	Children can use a mirror or tracing paper to help them with this question.

Answers

Question number	Answer	Mark	Parent's notes and additional comments
11a	Column of tally chart filled in as follows: 6 **14** **15** **7** **10** All answers must be correct.	1	
11b	52	1	
11c	Dean's row should show 15 shells.	1	
12	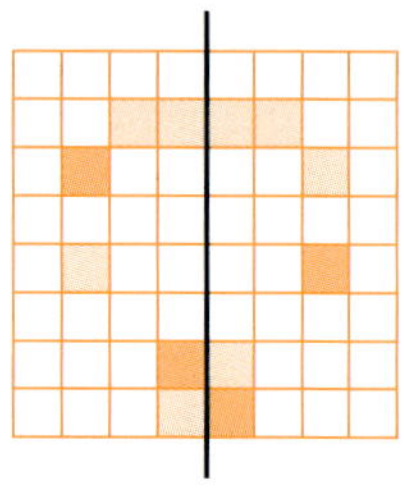	1	Children can use a mirror or tracing paper to help them with this question.
13	404	1	Any non-calculator method can be used to find the answer.
14	25	1	Any non-calculator method can be used to find the answer.
15	325 g	1	Mass is the correct word to use when finding how heavy something is on Earth. Children may have been using the word 'weight' instead of 'mass' in earlier years.
16	9	1	
17	A line drawn that is 7 cm long. Allow up to 2 mm for error.	1	
18	A ring around 3 drawing pins.	1	
19a	9765	1	Use number cards to practise this type of question. Give your child several cards and ask him or her to make two-, three- or four-digit numbers greater (more) than or less than a given number, or lying between two e.g. between 4000 and 6000. Ask him or her to make odd or even numbers or those divisible by 2, 5 or 10.
19b	5679	1	
19c	6795, 6975, 7695, 7965, 9765 *or* 9675	1	
19d	5796, 5769, 5976, 5967, 5679, 5697, 6975, 6957, 6795, 6759, 6579 *or* 6597	1	

Question number	Answer	Mark	Parent's notes and additional comments
20	804	1	Any non-calculator method can be used to find the answer.
21	483 → 500 648 → 600 591 → 600 353 → 400	1	Remind your child that numbers ending in 5 are rounded up.
22	£15.27	1	Note that amounts of money should never be written with both the **£** sign and a **p** sign, e.g. £15.27p is incorrect and would not earn a mark.
23	288, 144, **72, 36, 18**	1	
24	200 – (5 × 32)	1	
25	3700	1	
26	Any numbers of 50p and 20p coins totalling £7.60, e.g. 14 × 50p and 3 × 20p.	1	
27	Octagon (an eight-sided shape) with at least 1 right angle, e.g.: 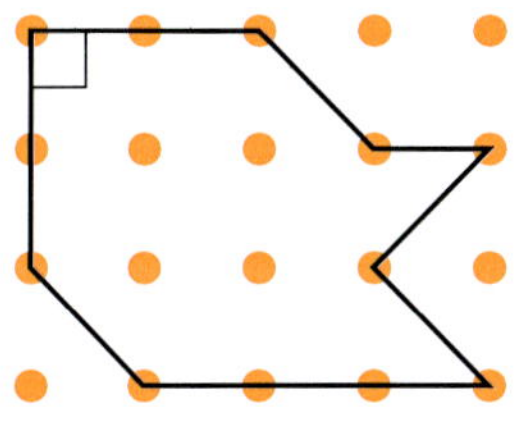	1	
28	2:55	1	Discuss the different ways of showing or describing the times on a clock, e.g. 7:40 can be described as 'seven forty', 'twenty to eight' or 'twenty minutes to eight' and can be shown on a traditional clock face or in digital form.
29	17 = 34 − 17 24 = 40 − 16 28 = 19 + 9 38 = 52 − 14 46 = 37 + 9 43 = 28 + 15 Award one mark if all but two matches are correct.	2	
30	Any 2 squares of the grid shaded. (Award a mark if part squares are shaded provided the total is 2 squares.)	1	One tenth of 20 squares is 2 squares. Encourage your child to find one tenth by dividing by 10.
31	12	1	
32	It is a hexagon with one right angle.	1	

Answers

Part B

Question number	Answer	Mark	Parent's notes and additional comments
33	36	1	Any non-calculator method can be used to find the answer.
34	56	1	A multiple is a number that can be exactly divided by another with no remainder.
35	2.9	1	A useful way of finding the number half way between two others is to add the two numbers, e.g. 2.6 and 3.2, and then halve the answer, e.g. $5.8 \div 2 = 2.9$
36a	The new corners (vertices) must be positioned at (4, 2) and (7, 5).	1	
36b	(1, 5) (4, 8) (7, 5) (4, 2) These co-ordinates can be written in any order. Award one mark if only one is incorrect.	2	Remind your child that the first co-ordinate tells you how many across and the second tells you how many up (or down). Use the phrase 'Into the house and up the stairs' to help your child remember the order.
37a		1	
37b	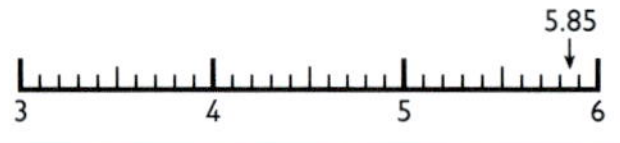	1	
38	1, 2, **3, 6, 9, 18** The numbers can be in any order.	1	A factor is a number that can divide exactly into another with no remainder, e.g. 4 is a factor of 8.
39	150 g	1	
40	10 hours 39 minutes	1	Here children are required to be familiar with the twenty-four hour clock.
41	$37 - 29 = 24 \div$ **3**	1	Children sometimes make mistakes with this type of question as they do not fully understand the meaning of the equals sign (=). Some children incorrectly view it as an 'answer giver' and will say that 37 – 29 does not give the answer 24. Show your child that the equals sign stands for 'is the same value as', to demonstrate that the answer to one side of the number sentence is the same as the answer to the other side.
42	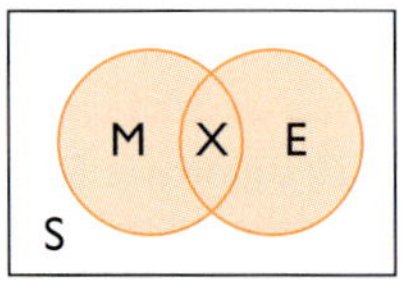 Award 1 mark if three out of four letters are correctly positioned.	2	
43	42 cm^2	1	The perimeter is the distance all the way around the shape. If the perimeter is 26 cm, then the total of the four sides is 26 cm, so if one side is 6 cm, the other must be 7 cm. To find the area of a rectangle, multiply the length (7 cm) by the width (6 cm) = 42 cm^2.
44a	16	1	
44b	15	1	

Answers

Mental Maths Test

1 18

2 12

3 3

4 22

5 43, 45, 47 *or* 49

6 1000 *or* one thousand

7 12

8 27

9 712

10 1.1

11 106

12 £1.20 *or* 120p

13 Any two numbers with a difference of 16, e.g. 1 and 17, 15 and 31 etc.

14 24

15 10 cm

16 12

17 250 cm

18 50

19 0.9

20 60

National Curriculum Levels

The test in Year 4 has a part A and a part B.

The score is out of a maximum of 59 marks (42 marks for Part A and 17 for part B).
If your child has scored highly in Part A, he or she can go on to try the harder questions in part B.

Write your child's scores below:

Mark scored in Part A

Mark scored in Part B

Total

Children at Year 4 complete a test of this type and from this each child can be levelled and graded according to his or her total score. The children do not sit a formal Mental Maths test at this stage.

Total marks 59

Mark	0-10	11–15	16–20	21–26	27–31	32–36	37–41	42–59
Level	**Below Level 2**	**Level 2C**	**Level 2B**	**Level 2A**	**Level 3C**	**Level 3B**	**Level 3A**	**Level 4**

If a child scores very highly on the test, there is a possibility of sitting the Year 5 or 6 tests, to gain clearer information about the extent to which he or she is performing at Level 4.

NUMBER AND ALGEBRA

1 Find the answers:

$57 + 14 =$	$28 + 79 =$
$189 + 245 =$	$134 + 749 =$
$91 - 38 =$	$82 - 43 =$
$778 - 364 =$	$626 - 389 =$
$8 \times 3 =$	$6 \times 4 =$
$13 \times 3 =$	$15 \times 5 =$
$27 \div 3 =$	$35 \div 5 =$
$36 \div 4 =$	$36 \div 3 =$

2 Fill in the missing signs. $+$ $-$ $\times$ $\div$

16 ◯ 4 = 4	34 ◯ 28 = 6
125 ◯ 25 = 150	14 ◯ 3 = 42
100 ◯ 25 = 4	103 ◯ 5 = 98
24 ◯ 1 ◯ 5 = 5	
33 ◯ 3 ◯ 5 = 6	

NUMBER AND ALGEBRA

3 Fill in the missing numbers.

$27 \div \square = 3$

$4 \times \square = 44$

$37 - 11 = 15 + \square$

$6 + 27 = 40 - \square$

4 Continue these patterns:

3, 6, 9, 12, ☐ ☐ ☐

95, 96, 97, 98, ☐ ☐ ☐

0, 25, 50, 75, ☐ ☐ ☐

212, 211, 210, ☐ ☐ ☐

4002, 4001, 4000, ☐ ☐ ☐

NUMBER AND ALGEBRA

5 **Halve:**

18	26	70
120	68	150
52	78	144

Double:

8	12	25
40	150	34
72	59	135

6 Answer these worded questions.

A magazine costs £1.20.
How much does it cost for two magazines? £

A camera film costs £3.68.
How much does it cost for two films? £

24 eggs are put into boxes of six.
How many boxes will be filled? boxes

How many 20 cm lengths of ribbon can be cut from a length of 100 cm? lengths

I have 66 pence. How many 6p chews can I buy? chews

SHAPE, SPACE AND MEASURES

7 Shade four more squares to make this pattern symmetrical.

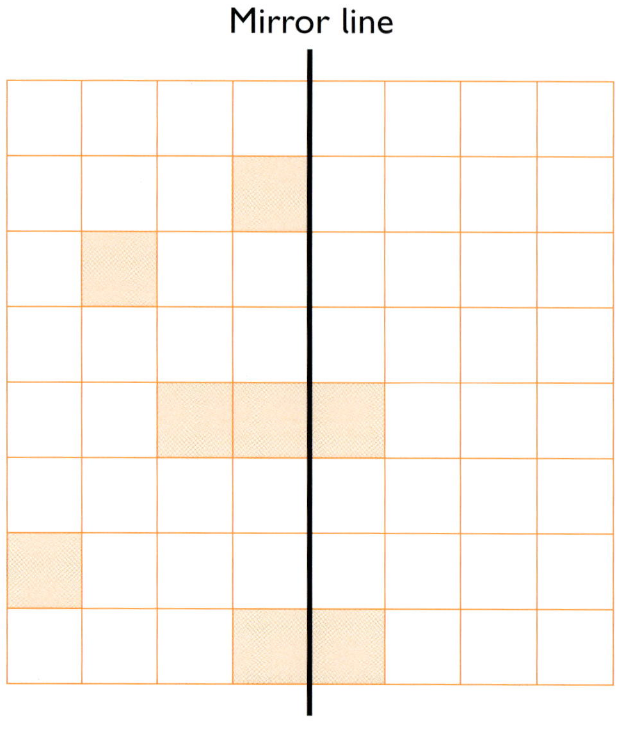

8 Draw and label a **hexagon**, a **pentagon** and an **octagon** on this grid.

SHAPE, SPACE AND MEASURES

9 Write the times on these clocks in digital form.

: : : :

10 Draw the hands of the clocks to show these times.

1:30 8:15 11:35 6:50

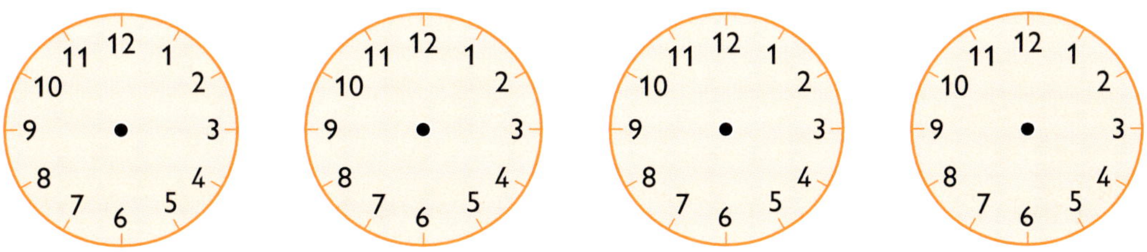

11 Which numbers are the arrows pointing to?

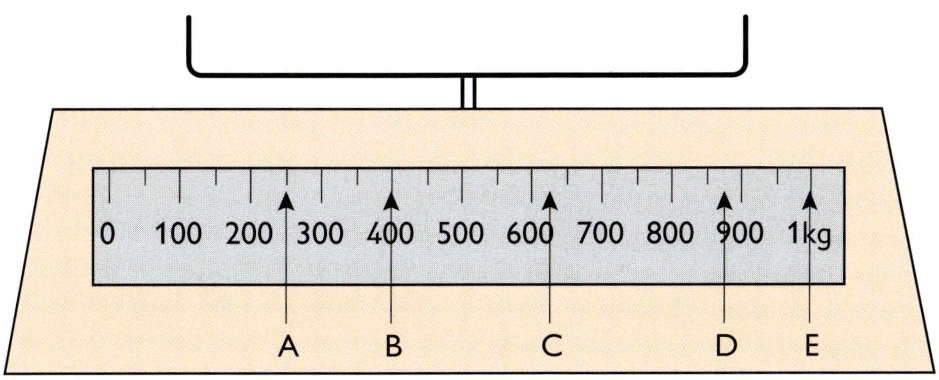

A B C D E

Answers

Practice Pages

1

71	107
434	883
53	39
414	237
24	24
39	75
9	7
9	12

2

÷	−
+	×
÷	−
+, ÷	
−, ÷	

3 9
11
11
7

4 15, 18, 21
99, 100, 101
100, 125, 150
209, 208, 207
3999, 3998, 3997

5

9	13	35
60	34	75
26	39	72
16	24	50
80	300	68
144	118	270

6 £2.40
£7.36
4
5
11

7

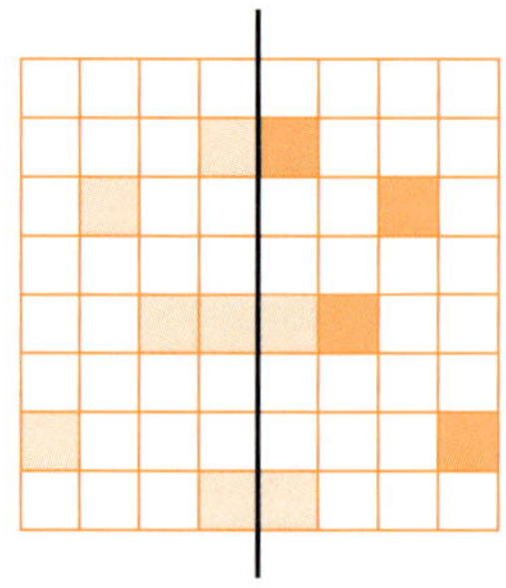

8 Labelled hexagon (6 straight sides)
Labelled pentagon (5 straight sides)
Labelled octagon (8 straight sides)

9 12:15 4:30 7:20 10:55
(or in 24-hour clock time)

10

11 250 g, 400 g, 625 g, 875 g,
1 kg (or 1000 g)

Notes